My First Book of
Animals

ALL ABOUT THE WORLD'S
WILDLIFE FOR KIDS

SARAH BARNETT, MA

ROCKRIDGE
PRESS

For my boys, Leo and Dean.

For general information on our other products and services, please contact our Customer Care Department within the United States at (866) 744-2665, or outside the United States at (510) 253-0500.

Hardcover ISBN: 979-8-88608-915-8
Paperback ISBN: 978-1-68539-555-1
eBook ISBN: 979-8-88608-301-9

Manufactured in the United States of America

Series Designer: Sean Doyle
Interior and Cover Designer: Alex Klawitter
Art Producer: Megan Baggott
Editor: Laura Bryn Sisson
Production Editor: Cassie Gitkin
Production Manager: Martin Worthington

Photography © iStock, cover and pp. 13, 22, 23, 26, 29, 33, 44; Robert Harding/Alamy Stock Photo, p. 34; Nature Picture Library/Alamy Stock Photo, p. 39; Francois Gohier/VWPics/Alamy Stock Photo, p. 47; All other images used under license from Shutterstock.

10 9 8 7 6 5 4 3 2 1 0

This book belongs to:

_____

What Is an Animal?

We share our planet with animals. Animals live in every corner of the earth.

An animal is a **living thing**. Animals are different from plants and **fungi**. Animals can move from one place to another on their own.

Animals come in many different shapes and sizes, but they all have things in common. They can move (walk, swim, fly, or slither), breathe (with lungs or gills), and make babies (by eggs or birth)!

King Penguins

All animals have special body parts that help them live in their habitat. A habitat is an animal's home. Animals find food, water, and shelter in their habitat.

The Animal Kingdom

What do you have in common with elephants, snakes, penguins, and jellyfish? You all belong to the same kingdom of living things: the animal kingdom.

All animals are a part of the animal kingdom. The animal kingdom includes almost nine million species that we know of. Species are a group of similar living things.

Jellyfish

Some animals on Earth are **amphibians**. The word "amphibian" means "two lives"—one on land and one in water. These animals can live in both places!

Red-Eyed Tree Frog

The animal kingdom is incredibly diverse. The animals in it can be very different from one another. This includes tiny frogs to huge whales!

Are you ready to learn about some of the most fascinating animals? We will learn about **mammals**, **reptiles**, **birds**, **fish**, amphibians, and even **invertebrates**!

Elephants

Elephants are the largest land mammals and are gentle and smart.

They have large, thin ears that help cool them down and long, powerful trunks.

An elephant's trunk is more than a nose. Elephants use their trunks to play and give hugs, pick up food, and suck up water. An elephant's trunk can weigh three hundred pounds!

Type: Mammal

Habitat: Savannas, grasslands, and forests in parts of Africa and Asia

Food: Roots, grass, fruit, bark

Size: 18–24 feet (trunk to tail); 4,000–24,000 pounds

Rhinoceros

Rhinos are known for their giant horns. The name "rhinoceros" actually means "nose horn."

Rhinos are very large and strong, and they only eat plants and grass for food. They are **herbivores**.

If you see a rhino, you may see its special bird friend—an oxpecker—living on its body!

Type: Mammal

Habitat: Grasslands, savannas, shrublands, forests and deserts in parts of Africa and Asia

Food: Grass, shrubs, trees, bark

Size: 7.8—15 feet long; 1,320–10,000 pounds

Hippos

There are two kinds of hippos: common and pygmy.

A common hippo can weigh as much as four cows!
A pygmy hippo can weigh the same as a big pig.

Hippos are nocturnal. That means they sleep all day
and stay up all night. At night, they look for food.

Type: Mammal

**Habitat: Near slow-moving rivers and lakes in
parts of Africa**

Food: Grass, leaves, fruit, water plants

Size: 4.9–16.5 feet long; 600–9,920 pounds

Type: Mammal

Habitat: Grasslands and plains in parts of Africa and India

Food: Buffalo, zebras, giraffes, warthogs, antelope

Size: 4.6–8.3 feet long; 270–570 pounds

Lions

The lion is known as the "king of the beasts." Lions are strong and brave.

Lions, like pet cats, can spend at least twenty hours a day resting.

Unlike most big cats, lions like to live in groups called prides.

Male lions have a bushy mane around their head. Their manes show other lions how strong and healthy they are.

Tigers

Tigers are enormous. They are the largest cats in the world.

The tiger is the only wildcat that has stripes. Each tiger's stripe pattern is different.

Most tigers live alone. As a tiger walks around, it scratches trees and leaves smells behind. Other tigers see or smell these clues to know who lives there.

Type: Mammal

Habitat: Rain forests, grasslands, savannas, and mangrove swamps in parts of Asia

Food: Deer, wild pigs, water buffalo, antelope

Size: 7–10 feet (head to tail); 205–680 pounds

Cheetahs

Cheetahs are the fastest land mammals on Earth. They run so fast that they look like they are flying!

Cheetahs have "tear marks" that run from their eyes to their mouth. The spots on their fur look like polka dots.

To communicate, cheetahs bark, chirp, and purr! They do not roar.

Type: **Mammal**

Habitat: **Grasslands of Africa and Asia**

Food: **Small antelope, impala, gazelles, warthogs, birds, rabbits**

Size: **body: 3.7–4.6 feet; tail: 2–2.7 feet; 77–143 pounds**

Bears

There are eight different kinds of bears. Some bears have brown or black fur, and polar bears have white fur. It helps them hide in the snow.

Bears have large bodies, but that doesn't slow them down! They can run very fast and are also good at climbing and swimming.

Type: Mammal

Habitat: Forests, mountains, tundra, deserts, and grassy areas

Food: Berries, roots, nuts, fish, birds

Size: 4–10 feet tall; 60–1,600 pounds

Brown bears

Bears are great swimmers. They can swim better than humans. Polar bears can swim the best. They can swim a very long time without stopping!

Bears have a large brain and are one of the smartest mammals. They can even see in color—something that most mammals cannot do.

Pandas are bears, too. They munch on **bamboo** stems and leaves most of the day. Male pandas sometimes do handstands next to trees to relax!

Wolves

Owoooo! Wolves use sounds to communicate. Wolf pups start to howl when they are just two weeks old.

Wolves look a lot like dogs, but they are not pets. They roam forests, deserts, and mountains. They are dangerous.

To eat, wolves hunt in packs. They sniff out food from far away.

Type: Mammal

Habitat: Many different habitats in North America and Eurasia

Food: Deer, elk, bison, moose, beavers, rodents

Size: 3.4–5.2 feet (head to tail); 50–180 pounds

Type: Mammal

Habitat: Forests and grasslands in Africa, Asia, Central America, and South America

Food: Fruits, nuts, lizards, bird eggs

Size: 4 inches–3.3 feet; 3.5 ounces–79 pounds

Monkeys

Look! There's a monkey in that tree!

Monkeys and humans are **primates**. Primates are some of the smartest animals.

Monkeys have hands and feet like ours. They hold on to things with them.

Almost all monkeys (except apes) have tails. Their tails help them balance. They can also use their tails to hold things and hang on branches.

There are about 260 different types of monkeys. Some live in trees, and others live on the ground.

Monkeys live in groups called troops. Troop members eat, play, and sleep together. They also groom one another. They pick out insects, dirt, and seeds from each other's hair.

The howler monkey can howl so loud that it can be heard from up to three miles away. They are one of the loudest land mammals!

Gorillas

A gorilla is an ape. Apes are primates.

Gorillas are large but gentle animals. They can express sadness, joy, fear, and confusion on their faces. They make sounds to communicate.

Gorillas spend most of their time eating and sleeping. Adult gorillas eat up to sixty pounds of food each day!

Type: Mammal

Habitat: Forests of Central and Western Africa

Food: Bamboo, wild celery, thistles, flowers, fruit, bark

Size: 4–6 feet; 150–500 pounds

Kangaroos

Kangaroos are **marsupials**, a type of mammal. Marsupial mothers have a pouch for their baby.

The kangaroo is the only large animal that hops everywhere. Kangaroos have short front legs, strong back legs, large back feet, and powerful tails. Their tails help them balance.

Kangaroos are great jumpers. They can leap as far as 30 feet!

Type: Mammal

Habitat: Deserts, grasslands, and forests in Australia and nearby islands

Food: Grass, leaves, other plants

Size: 6 inches–6 feet; 12 ounces–200 pounds

Sloths

Shh! The sloth is sleeping! This drowsy mammal sleeps most of the day and moves very slowly when awake.

Sloths live high up in the trees and rarely come down. They hang for hours using their long arms. Once a week, sloths climb down to the forest floor to poop!

Type: Mammal

Habitat: Tropical rain forests in Central and South America

Food: Leaves, twigs, buds

Size: 2–2.5 feet; 9–17 pounds

Snakes

Guess what animal is long, round, and slides on the ground? It has a tongue that flicks and eyes that can't blink.

Type: **Reptile**

Habitat: **Many different habitats across all continents except Antarctica**

Food: **Small mammals, birds, insects, amphibians**

Size: **4 inches–30 feet; .02 ounce–550 pounds**

Did you guess a snake? You're right!

Snakes move very well without legs. They use their entire bodies to get from place to place.

A snake's tongue is forked. Instead of using their tongue to taste, snakes use it to smell. They flick it in and out to catch smells. They spread the forked part out to know which direction the smell is coming from.

Snakes' ears are deep inside their heads. Sound travels through the snakes' bones for them to hear!

Some people think the skin of a snake will feel damp and slimy. But a snake's skin actually feels dry and soft.

Type: **Amphibian**

Habitat: **In fresh water on every continent except Antarctica**

Food: **Crickets, worms, caterpillars, flies, grasshoppers**

Size: **0.3–16.7 inches; 0.3–98 ounces**

Frogs

Frogs are amphibians. They are cold-blooded.

Frogs need water but do not drink it. Instead, they absorb it through their skin.

Some frogs can lay twenty thousand eggs at one time. Can you imagine having thousands of brothers and sisters?

When frog eggs hatch, they are called tadpoles. Tadpoles look very different from adult frogs.

Crocodiles

Crocodiles are the largest reptiles on Earth. All reptiles have tails. Crocodiles use theirs to swim fast.

A crocodile can easily sneak up on **prey** by swimming with only its eyes, ears, and nose showing above the water.

Crocodiles don't sweat. They open their mouths to cool off, like a dog!

Type: **Reptile**

Habitat: **In warm waters in many parts of the world**

Food: **Insects, fish, small frogs, lizards, small mammals**

Size: **10–20 feet; 330–2,205 pounds**

Whales

Whales are the mighty giants of the ocean. They are marine mammals.

A whale has a long body shaped like a rocket. Its fins and tail help it swim.

Whales cannot breathe underwater. To breathe, they swim up to the surface and send air through their blowhole. Then they breathe in more air.

Type: Mammal

Habitat: In oceans all over the world

Food: Squid, octopus, crustaceans, fish, seals, sharks, birds

Size: 5–105 feet; 400–440,000 pounds

When whales jump out of the water, they are breaching. When humpback whales breach, they may be sending messages to other whales.

Some whales, like blue whales, have baleen instead of teeth. Baleen looks like broomlike bristles. Bits of tiny food called krill get trapped on it for the whale to eat.

Whales live longer on average than all other mammals. The bowhead whale lives the longest—up to two hundred years!

Blue whales are the biggest animals that have ever lived—even bigger than dinosaurs! They can grow as long as three school buses put together and can weigh as much as thirty elephants.

Type: Fish

Habitat: In water all over the Earth

Food: Fish, crustaceans, mollusks, marine mammals, other sharks

Size: 6 inches–62 feet; half an ounce–21 tons

Sharks

Some people think sharks are scary and dangerous to humans. But sharks actually don't hurt people very often.

Sharks have been on Earth since long before dinosaurs. They are great hunters and very fast swimmers.

Did you know that sharks don't have bones? Their skeletons are made of cartilage, which is softer than bone.

Sharks have to keep swimming all the time. Otherwise, they would sink. They swim thousands of miles every year!

Sharks are picky eaters. They look like they are hungry and looking for food all the time, but that's not true. They only eat one small meal every two or three days.

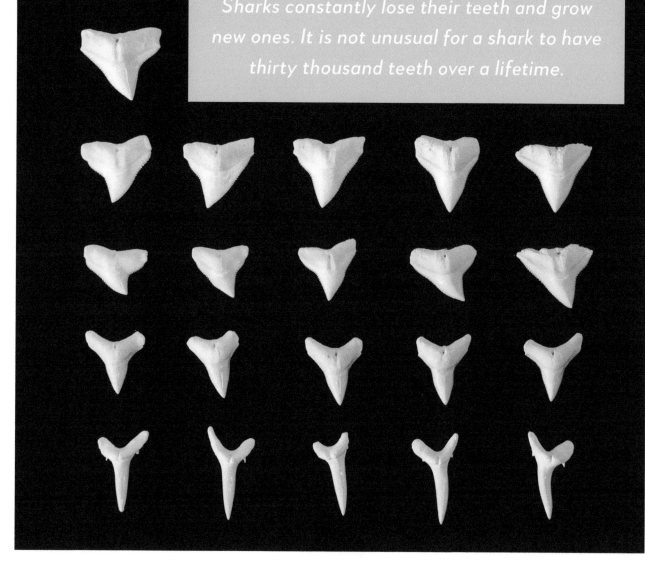

Sharks constantly lose their teeth and grow new ones. It is not unusual for a shark to have thirty thousand teeth over a lifetime.

Octopus

Octopuses are smart and special animals.

They can change colors quickly and twist their bodies into shapes. They squirt clouds of ink, have three hearts, and have blue blood!

Octopuses have eight arms that are attached to their heads.

They are invertebrates, or animals without bones. Even large octopuses can squeeze through tiny holes!

Type: **Invertebrate**

Habitat: **All Earth's seas and oceans**

Food: **Shrimp, lobsters, crabs, snails, clams**

Size: **1 inch–20 feet; 1 gram–110 pounds**

Jellyfish

Don't let their name fool you. Jellyfish are not actually fish! They are a type of **plankton**.

Jellyfish are invertebrates. Like other invertebrates, they do not have bones. They also do not have blood or a brain.

Jellyfish bodies are usually clear. Some are brightly colored, and some even glow!

Type: Invertebrate

Habitat: In oceans all over the Earth

Food: Shrimp, krill, small fish

Size: 1 centimeter–120 feet;
2 ounces–200 pounds

Type: **Bird**

Habitat: **Between the Equator and South Pole—always by water**

Food: **Krill, squid, and fish**

Size: **15 inches–4 feet; 2–90 pounds**

Penguins

Penguins are birds that swim underwater. They cannot fly.

When penguins walk, they waddle. They have short legs.

Most penguins live in a large colony with thousands or even millions of other penguins. They huddle to stay warm.

Some penguins sleep standing up. Penguins can also sleep in the water!

Owls

An owl is a kind of bird called a **raptor**. Raptors hunt small animals for food.

Most owls are nocturnal. They are active at night.

Many owls see very well in the dark. They cannot move their big round eyes like people can. They must move their head to see in other directions.

Type: **Bird**

Habitat: **Almost everywhere in the world, especially in woodlands**

Food: **Insects, fish, reptiles, amphibians, birds, small mammals**

Size: **5–26 inches; 1.5 ounces–9 pounds**

Animals and You

This book is only the beginning. Earth still holds surprises for scientists and people. There are always new animals to discover and learn about.

Did you know that some animals need our help? You can help animals and their habitats by **recycling**, cleaning up land, and learning more about them!

GLOSSARY

AMPHIBIAN: A cold-blooded animal that can live on land and in water

ANIMAL KINGDOM: A group of natural objects that includes all living and extinct animals

BAMBOO: A type of tall, treelike grass

BIRD: Vertebrate animals that have feathers, wings, and beaks

CARTILAGE: A bendable material that is softer than bone

FISH: An animal that lives in water and has fins for swimming and gills for breathing

FUNGI: A group of living organisms that reproduce by spores

GILLS: An organ a fish uses to take in oxygen from water

GRASSLAND: Land filled with low-growing plants such as grasses and wildflowers

HABITAT: The place or environment where an animal naturally lives

HERBIVORE: An animal that only eats plants

INVERTEBRATE: An animal without a backbone

KRILL: Tiny animals that are similar to shrimp

LIVING THING: Things that are now or once were alive

MAMMAL: A warm-blooded animal that has hair or fur and

feeds its young milk; most give birth to live young

MANGROVE SWAMP: A woodland or shrubland habitat formed by mangrove trees

MARSUPIAL: A group of mammals that are known for carrying their young in a pouch

NOCTURNAL: Being active during the night

PLAINS: Large areas of land that are mostly flat

PLANKTON: An organism that is moved by tides and currents, and can't swim strongly against them. Many are too small to be seen by human eyes.

PREY: An animal that is hunted or killed by another animal for food

PRIMATE: A type of mammal that has good eyesight and flexible hands and feet

RAPTOR: A type of bird that hunts other animals for food

RECYCLING: Taking materials ready to be thrown away and changing them into reusable materials

REPTILE: A cold-blooded animal that has scaly skin; the majority lay soft-shelled eggs on land

SAVANNA: A flat plain covered with grass and scattered trees

SPECIES: A group of similar living things that can reproduce with one another

TUNDRA: A large, cold region with no trees

ABOUT THE AUTHOR

 **SARAH BARNETT**, MA, is a National Board Certified Teacher who has spent many years teaching kindergarten and first grade. In addition to teaching children, she also teaches teachers! She is the mom of two young boys, and together they love exploring and learning about new animals. Visit her online at mrsbteachesme.com.